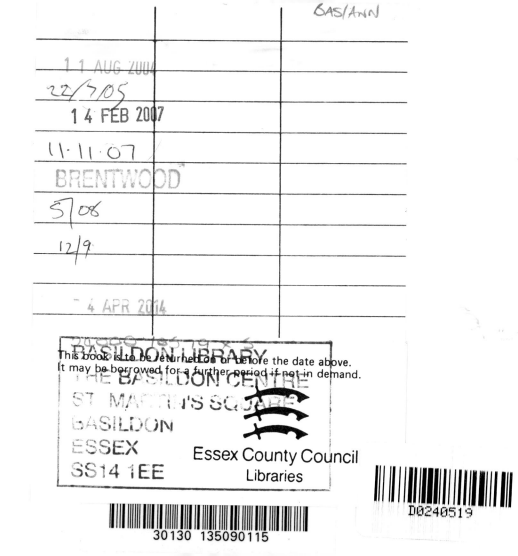

ALLOTMENT FOLK

CHRIS OPPERMAN

ALLOTMENT FOLK

CONTENTS

ALLOTMENTS AND ALLOTMENT FOLK

I learned to smoke on an allotment, and a chum enjoyed his first kiss among the seed trays and strawberry nets that had their home in "our" hut. I say "our" hut – it was a second home. Like William and the Outlaws, we'd lurk and plan, loiter and plot among the hoes, rakes, spades and dibbers.

We never met the owner, nor were we chased away by the other gardeners tending their crops. We weren't considered potential vandals or robbers. In fact, our presence might have been seen as some sort of security. We certainly enjoyed our unilateral assault on slugs, taking it upon ourselves to empty and recharge the various novel attempts to keep plots free of the slimy thieves. Like the battle with the elements, the war on slugs continues, testing the ingenuity of allotmenteers from one generation to the next.

My first legitimate foray on to the allotments was during Bob-a-Job Week. I was given some weeding to do, in full Cub uniform, for what turned out to be half a crown. I wasn't allowed a hoe. The allotmenteer was very wise: the combination of sharp blade and nine-year-old boy could have seen off the fruit of hours of labour in seconds. With the silver came a bunch of greens for the family pot and a love of growing and rearing.

The allotments are still there along with what I like to think is the hut that hid the packet of Park Drive filter tips and harboured so many other boyish secrets. It has drooped and sagged and settled into a cosy state of indestructibility, rather like the older generation of allotmenteers, the "old boys", who are always willing – and secretly, delighted – to offer advice to the new wave of men and women, and young families, who are gradually returning to their roots.

As a somewhat jaundiced adult looking back on those days of innocence – apart from those few illicit ciggies that put us off for life – it is heartening to see allotment power is taking hold and in some cases halting the march of the brick-built rabbit hutch. Developers are being told they can forget their plans to plant rows of terraces where for decades or even centuries there have been rows of potatoes and carrots.

Indeed, the allotment is enjoying a revival. Turning our backs on geometric decking and bladder-tickling water features, more of us are returning to reap a harvest from the land, and falling in love all over again. Extroverts dig and decorate and allow their inner person to flourish on and in the earth, quiet turners of the soil get on with communing with nature, livestock thrives in an atmosphere of growing and caring, the organic grower tests the old ways and experiments with the new, the intensive operator uses hi-tech gadgetry and chemicals to fill the barrow with goodies for the kitchen, and the flower person has a house full of colour the whole year round.

A POTTED HISTORY OF THE PLOT

8

The word "allotment" belies the spirit and enterprise that goes into the 10 rods, which make up the standard allotment. That 250m^2 of backache and bounty deserves something better. However, its history is more interesting.

Although there are some small Celtic fields in Cornwall that are used as allotments today, we have to go back to Anglo-Saxon times to discover the first "allotted" pieces of land. The

community cleared the woodland that covered much of the country, then it was shared out.

The allotment, in its infancy, was seen more as a means of survival than as recreation or an alternative to the supermarket. This was certainly the case from the reign of Elizabeth I, when manorial common land was enclosed and commoners were compensated with allotments of land attached to their cottages.

The early 19th century saw more enclosures, and by 1845 the fear of a peasant revolt led to the General Enclosures Act. Commissioners travelled the country authorising enclosures only on condition that land was set aside as allotments. However, the full weight of the law was often required to ensure there were enough plots to keep the working classes fed. In 1887 the Allotment Act saw to it that local authorities were obliged to provide allotments if there was a demand. Again, that wasn't enough. The local authorities still resisted until the Allotment Act of 1908 imposed responsibilities on parish, urban, district and borough councils to provide land for cultivation so long as it was not for commercial purposes. That rule still applies today.

Through both world wars the allotments proved their worth. As the U-boats sank our food lifeline so the allotments moved out of the exclusive use of the rural working classes. It became *de rigueur* to be "off to the allotment". WW2's "Dig for Victory" campaign saw parks and public gardens producing crops alongside the allotments and farms, but victory heralded a decline in the number of plots. From a peak in 1918 of 1.5 million we are now down to around 330,000 across the UK. Through the 1950s and 1960s many thousands of allotment acres fell into disuse and were snapped up by local authorities for development.

A GROWTH FUTURE

I like to think a healthy stock of well-run plots is a sign that through all the nastiness of today, there is still a desire to sow and reap. To bend the back to the soil, sow, prick out and grow on has an ageless thrill. It's a basic instinct too many people have denied themselves. Give children a yard or two of soil and a packet of seeds and watch them take to the land, watch them be natural. Allotments are not just for lonely old gits...

There is an age-old sense of camaraderie, trust and rivalry on the allotments, with characters from every walk of life – taxi-drivers and ex-miners to PR-gurus and performance artists – working away on everything from rows of tasty vegetables and beds of glorious blooms to ornamental ponds, pigeon lofts and patios, topiary and tobacco plants.

And, though the sights and sounds have moved into the 21st century, with CDs spinning and plastic bags cracking in the wind to keep off the feathered pilferers, even these have a simplicity worthy of the well-worn fork and spade, the much-loved trowel and the ubiquitous and multi-talented sheet of corrugated iron.

Long live the muck heap, the trim, grassed walkways and the wigwams of runner beans. May the marrows continue to win prizes and the dahlias, hearts. Here's to a very special set of people.

Chris Opperman

JUST WHAT I WANTED!

David won't forget Father's Day, five years ago, in a hurry. "My wife, Rachel, said she wanted to show me something on the allotments. We stopped at a plot head high in every weed you could think of and she said, 'What do you think of that? Happy Father's Day.' All I could manage was a doubtful 'Lovely.'"

In fact, the plot was so derelict they had the first six months rent-free. But they were hooked, managed to scratch a few beans out of the first year, then went on to win best-kept plot three years running. All this on Suffolk clay, which has been known to break spirits as well as backs.

A deep pond now reflects the marigolds, salvias and ageratums as David and Rachel take tea on the patio looking down to the immaculate rows of vegetables. "I never had a hobby before. Now, everything's gardening. I've been taken under the wing of an old boy of 80 as, at 52, I'm a young 'un on the plot."

"My mother-in-law bought me some leather gardening gloves, but I daren't wear them."

PARADISE ON EARTH

When Diahann and Malcolm sit taking tea and buns on the lawn in front of their chalet they're in a place that has special meaning for them. "It's been our lifeline, quite literally. Malcolm had a heart attack, he was very ill, and that was followed by being made redundant. He's not a person to sit about all day feeling sorry for himself so we took on this garden. It was the best thing we could have done."

Diahann and Malcolm's floral paradise sits among many others. Theirs is a chalet garden allotment site where the rules say there has to be a summerhouse rather than a shed, and plants, flowers, shrubs and lawns instead of vegetables. "Ponds are optional." And Diahann should know. She's the site representative on the plot, sorting out lettings and generally keeping an eye on things. "We have a grassed area for games, and even a toilet block... A nice change from the traditional bucket."

"As flat dwellers, it's our little heaven."

MARROWS GO METRIC

Les haunts the murky world of prize marrow growing. For 10 years, he, and wife, Irene, have worked their double plot, which has the luxury of being at the end of their garden. "Irene does the artistic bit. I get on with my heaps."

A marrow heap – if you can believe a champion grower who has nurtured a monster that weighed in at almost 18 pounds – is made up of "rubbish" kept under black plastic with four holes for the green and yellow beauties, and another four for the high-tech lemonade bottle watering system. So now you know. Les was pipped – excuse the pun – by just 100 grams last year. Had metrication infiltrated the marrow world? "I don't know about that. To me it's two packets of baccy."

Les kindly keeps an eye on the ladies of the allotments, who outnumber the men. "It's good to see so many. I put them right, you might say."

"A good heap is the secret."

DUCKS ARE THE BEE'S KNEES

John is torn between his ducks and his bees. He says he's a beekeeper at heart, and, with 15 hives on his allotment – "too many really" – producing around 300 pounds of honey a year, he might just be right. But get John talking ducks and he's an equally happy man.

"I needed something to keep the grass down. Bees don't like strimmers and things, hens make bad neighbours but – ah! – ducks, they don't fly away and they pull up the grass nicely." John now has 14 quacking friends – Aylesburys and Khaki Campbells. "The children come and feed them, some in pushchairs, and the ducks act like a load of monks – always out with their begging bowls. They're not daft and they're always friendly and gentle."

The ducks get a break from gardening each August when John takes the hives out on to the moor for the bees to gorge on the heather. Then it's back to the allotment and their feathered friends.

"Hens are ignorant. Ducks are affectionate."

DON'T MENTION EUROPE

At 88, Frank has had to call it a day on his beloved allotment, but his knowledge gained over fifty years of tending his plot is going for free at the shop he helps run for allotment club members. Forty of those years were spent on the "same little bit of England", where Frank reckons he knew every slug by name.

Frank laughs a lot. He has to, otherwise the rules and regulations of modern gardening would have him in tears. "They're even thinking of getting rid of Jeye's fluid." Oh, and don't mention gardening on the television. He says it ignores the basic principles of growing he learned when he was set free from the slums on to a garden and then an allotment.

Frank's first three words of advice to newcomers to the allotment shop are: "Dig and weed." If that doesn't scare them off, he adds, "And be patient." Then he laughs.

"We're thinking of becoming an EU-free zone."

JUST WHAT THE DOCTOR ORDERED

Kathryn's allotment has changed her life. She's an agoraphobic and has used the tranquillity and industry of the plot to enjoy the great outdoors at last. "At my worst I couldn't leave my bedroom. I still get panic attacks but the allotment is so relaxing, so calm. You get so involved in what you're doing it takes you out of yourself."

At 19, Kathryn is the youngest on the allotments. She and boyfriend Mike are into their first season and welcome all the support they get from the old hands. "My friends think I'm quite strange digging away on an allotment, but I don't care."

"Huge" pumpkins are the stars of the plot, along with organically grown vegetables and a corrugated iron shed that resembles a four-man-sentry-box-cum-bombshelter. "The floral curtains really set it off." And, if you have some time to kill, ask Kathryn about the compost heap.

22

"We'll be very popular in an air raid."

FROM CABBAGES TO WILD THINGS

The frosted stalks of sprouts looked like hastily left grave markers on a muddy battlefield. They got Gordon thinking. He turned his back on the sadness of his allotment in winter, with its abandoned Brussels and decomposing cabbages, and decided it should be nature's own colour-card all year round.

The plot became Gordon's enchanted garden. It won a prize for being the most wildlife-friendly in the area. And the bridged ponds, trees and flowers that flourish under Gordon's dedicated hand soon had queues of human visitors too.

Wife, Eunice, reckons she used to be pub widow. She got a job there to be near him – "love at first sip" – and is now an allotment widow – "at least I know where he is". Their bungalow plot is paved over. "Garden at home and you garden alone. The camaraderie is a huge part of the fun. We come from every conceivable walk of life."

"Allotments are great levellers."

MIND THE PLESIOSAURUS!

Mind you, you could hardly miss it. This "fishy dinosaur" is 18 feet long, the prize exhibit in Bernard's gallery of wooden sculptures that add art and imagination to his and Jenny's allotment.

He doesn't do much carving but he does have a great imagination. "I've got these lumps of iron-hard oak. Where bits have rotted away you're left with shapes that leave themselves open to lots of different interpretations. But my gnu, goat, albatross and plesiosaurus really jump out at you, if you see what I mean." Meanwhile, Bernard and Jenny have dedicated their four allotments to the celebration of nature and encouraging youngsters to enjoy "the countryside in the town."

Their prize winning eco-friendly plot is host to 26 species of birds and countless slow worms, lizards, voles and hedgehogs… And dozens of nature-mad townschildren. "A newborn baby was brought here. You could call it baptism by nature."

"Teach the young to respect nature
and we can't go far wrong."

I CAN'T AFFORD A CARRIAGE...

When Dickie shows his dahlias, they travel in style – in a top of the range, all bells and whistles, two-wheeled barrow. "We really put the others in the shade when Olive and I turn up with our blooms." Dickie's chesty laugh matches his rich sense of humour. He's addicted to dahlias. "It's like smoking. Once you start, you can't give up. The colours are fantastic, a pity they're so short-lived."

Dickie's base camp is impressive, a huge shed that used to be his brother's garage. A look inside and it's an Aladdin's Cave. Air-conditioning comes with the gaps in the planks. "You could say it's grown up with us..." More like fallen down. But it's home to a collection of miner's lamps that remind 79-year-old Dickie of his time down the pit, along with the bits and pieces collected over 50 years on the same allotment.

And wife, Olive, plays her part. She arranges the show blooms, sorts out the numbering... oh, and helps push the barrow.

"We win a prize or two... now and again."

...AND THREE ONION BHAJIS

There's a karahi at the bottom of Dhundi Raj's allotment. It takes pride of place in the shed among the spades, hoes, rakes and children's toys. Over three years, Dhundi Raj and Natasha – with three-year-old East directing from his swing – have created an outdoor playground, larder and kitchen. "We have a different world here. We work and play, growing organic food and cooking it."

That's where the karahi comes in – it's a Nepali wok. Dhundi Raj is from Nepal, where he was a farmer and restaurateur. Cooking Nepali and Indian food, surrounded by the fruits of the family's labour, is his idea of heaven.

Allotment life revolves around a huge apple tree, a fine shed, rows of much loved vegetables, fruit trees, bushes... and East's swing. "He knows the names of some of the plants. Learning about nature is so important." The slugs and snails try to spoil things, but "marigolds and onions keep most of them away."

"There are some wonderful smells."

BACK TO NATURE

A cross between an anarchist and a Buddhist, Ron is nature's champion. He took an allotment, saw to it that the rules were broken and created a perennial fruiting garden. "There was a regulation. Only vegetables. You couldn't even grow flowers. So we got things changed."

That was 11 years ago and now, at 55, Ron has found his place to "drop out". With an ancient hedgerow of blackthorn, elder and oak as a backcloth, it's an organic orchard, fruit garden, and a wild flower and animal haven. There are cobnuts up high, then pears, plums and apples, and meadow cranesbill, woundwort and celandine with raspberries and strawberries "as they fancy". "I call it vegan-organic. It's a spiritual place, not driven by the intensity of annuals."

Ron revels in the plot being low-maintenance – "although my wife, Ane is great with the pruning shears."

"I see an allotment as a place of deeper meaning."

WHEN YOU WISH UPON A STAR...

Walt Disney would have had a field day on Mark and Chris's London allotment. A fantasia of colour, or, as Mark puts it, "Some structure but with freestyle colour." That's his PR-agency speak for higgledy-piggledy vegetables and soft fruits, with sunflowers, marigolds, daturas and bronze fennel dotted among them.

And so, when it comes to potatoes, you would hardly expect Mark and Chris to stick just to reds and whites. They have blues and maroons, too, and their yellow courgettes and tummelberries vie with cardoons, aubergines, squashes, jostaberries and yams.

For five years, the gardeners have got off the Tube on their way home to work the plot on a summer's evening. "It's an urban idyll surrounded by mature trees, with geese flying over from the marshes." Their neighbours have dubbed the circular herb garden, with its radiating paths "the helipad" – an acknowledgement of Mark and Chris's eccentric and colourful contribution to the London scene.

"We're not into old-git-style rows."

LOOKING TO THE FUTURE

They're called ideal allotments – a perfect description. No fences between plots, youngsters encouraged to get involved and, in pride of place, a summerhouse-cum-meeting room with its own planted patio. It's the way ahead for communities wanting to turn their hands to the soil again and enjoy the great outdoors.

Overlooking the 65 plots that see the "insomniacs" digging and hoeing as early as five in the morning is this glass-fronted pavilion, which would do justice to a well-heeled cricket club. "We've got to hand it to Newcastle. They're trying hard with their 'Allotments and Leisure' to keep the plots alive. They built our HQ, which also has a children's play area."

Phil and the crew – John, Jed and Derek – are working on a wildlife area for the youngsters, with a pond and greenhouse. Just one snag. "Trying to find a clean mug in the sink can be a problem."

"The children are the allotmenteers of the future."

"WHEN YOU'RE SMILING...

...the flowers smile with you," says Freda. And Freda's smiles are brave ones. Even though she's in a bad way with arthritis she makes a point of getting to the allotment almost every day to tend her flowers, an extensive vegetable plot and two giant Christmas trees. She laughs. "The legs are bad but if you sit at home you go old and grey. I've gone white but I still have green fingers!"

Freda describes herself as a German lass, "although that was a long time ago" when she was one of 13 children and had to learn how to feed the family. "Vegetable growing is in the blood," she says. Unfortunately, Freda's husband wasn't interested in the plot she has tended for 20 years – "He didn't like mucky hands."

The allotment is a great comfort to Freda. Her pain is softened by the tea-drinking friendship there, and her other "friends", the dazzling banks of flowers.

"When you give up smiling, that's it."

GRAPES OF WRATH

Watch out for Chateau Duxford, a wine to note for the future. If it matches the struggle that resulted in its planting, it'll be a full-bodied affair with plenty of character... and a hint of raspberry.

Ian's miniature vineyard was born out of the parish council's decision to earmark the allotments for affordable housing. "We set up a fighting committee. It was a dogged campaign involving people from all walks of life including lawyers and senior civil servants." The battle saw occupancy of the plots rise to more than 80 per cent and the council retreated.

"I've planted 30 vines as a long-term crop, which need another three years. But while there's no wine-bearing fruit this year, we do have some first class raspberries growing alongside. They seem to delight in playing second fiddle to the grapes." Ian already has 50 bottles' worth of vines growing in his garden.

**"We've hung up our guns.
We're a management committee now."**

TALKING TO THE ANIMALS

There's nothing Derick – "They didn't know whether to call me Derek or Eric" – doesn't know about rabbits… or guinea pigs, or jackdaws, or ferrets. His prowess with finches earned him the nickname "Birdy", but nowadays "Doctor Dolittle" would be more appropriate. "As a youngster I used to tame jackdaws and sell them for five shillings each. I also kept foxes and finches and hens, ducks and geese."

Wife, Phyllis, also keeps rabbits on the allotment – "She's like me. Prefers animals to human beings." The plot is now home to 100 breeding rabbits, nine guinea pigs and some ferrets – "They're as soft as owt." He's currently in the process of saving for a new shed, "So's I can breed hamsters." When he's not grooming the stock, Derick does a "bit of everything".

And his little old dog is still on the scene. "Dinky died when she was 17. She's buried on the allotment in a proper coffin along with her toys."

"People who don't like animals are odd."

NEVER TRUST A SHOWMAN

Les retired as a mechanical engineer 15 years ago. "I caught up with all the jobs I had promised to do. Then Doreen, the wife, let me out to play." Les is now 80 and he reckons allotmenteering has taught him to be sly.

"A friend introduced me to showing. That was it. I became as bad as the rest. I have a four-foot cabbage but I keep it hidden and tell my mates I'm not showing. When they pop in for tea their eyes are everywhere. If they say they have nothing to show, you know they have."

When Les and his mates aren't hiding their mammoth marrows and oversize onions from one another, they dig for Food Futures, providing top class fruit and veg for a healthy eating campaign aimed at pensioners in and around Huddersfield. They are also building a polytunnel to let folk in wheelchairs enjoy growing their own food. "The allotment really is a new life."

"People who show are a cunning, conniving lot."

WITH MY ALLOTMENT I THEE WORSHIP

"Now let's be precise here. We've got three and a half allotments down to flowers and a half for vegetables." That's Geoff, who emphasises the "we", because if ever a love affair blossomed among the blooms it is his and Dot's. Their eyes met across neighbouring plots. Shy smiles soon flowered into hugs and kisses. And Geoff not only won the heart of Dot as they worked their flower beds, but also countless championships for his dahlias, chrysanthemums and, more recently, daffodils. He got into daffs "for something to do in the spring."

"Now we are together," says Dot, "so much so that when Geoff wins another first for whatever, I feel I've done it myself. It's lovely." Geoff even offered his precious spade to her as a love token. "I started my allotments in 1972. I still have the spade I bought then. There's not a lot of it left, but it handles beautifully for Dot." Only one thing blights this floral love affair. "We've run out of room for trophies."

"I don't grow my flowers to be second."

GOTTA LIGHT?

Chris smokes too much, coughs a bit, laughs a lot and talks forever. And his knowledge of *Nicotiana tobacum* is encyclopaedic. For six years, this semi-retired "they won't leave me alone" master upholsterer has tended tobacco on his allotment and now sells seeds, saving green-fingered smokers a fortune. "It's all quite legal so long as you don't try to sell or give away the finished product. Grow it for your own use and you're laughing," Chris coughs.

The facts and figures are mind-boggling: 500 plants on a reasonably well-maintained allotment – "I use soot from Kensington Palace" – will produce 100 kilos of tobacco. "At £185 a kilo, retail, that's a massive saving. You don't have to smoke it all at once. It matures with age, like wine." And that's 40-a-day Chris's other obsession. Alongside his orchard and pebble-dashed shed are vines that produce gallons of "good brew." His websites – www.coffinails.com (self explanatory) and www.fdw.com (falling down water) – sum him up quite nicely.

"They reckon I have verbal diarrhoea."

I DON'T KNOW WHY I LOVE YOU...

Mark loves his houseleeks. Once in a while these succulents – resembling spineless cacti – show their appreciation by bursting into tiny, vivid pink and yellow rosettes. They sit in their pots, set in gravel among the patio paving slabs, admired by fellow allotmenteers, including his father, Harry, pictured. "My dad has a plot on the same site. I got the 'bug' from him about three years ago."

Then Mark's passion for these unusual succulents was able to take off. The *Sempervivum* vie with the *Jovibarba*, and in the small greenhouse there are cacti. Like the houseleeks they're spineless and again, like their outdoor plot mates, they flower when they feel like it. "No, it's not frustrating. They look after themselves. That lets me get on with the vegetables on the rest of the allotment."

As a taxi driver, Mark can get on his plot a good three times a week. He agrees his interest in the fickle succulents might be considered odd. "But there's something about them."

"Don't ask me why they're called houseleeks."

SLUGS? YUMMY...

Incensed at the poisoning of the land by a local industrial estate, Paul vowed to put his money where his mouth was and create a wildlife refuge on a derelict allotment nearby.

Meter-reader Paul's hobby-cum-obsession is herpetology – the world of frogs, toads, lizards and newts. "I was so angry at what had happened. The estate had killed things off. The allotment was a tip of asbestos sheets and glass. I hadn't much money but I got a JCB, cleared things up and dug two ponds. You could almost hear the frogs say thank you."

Securely fenced, the allotment is home to newts and frogs in a watery world that is allowed to run wild. "I was living in a flat then. I had to have a green space I could mould. This was it." And there's a bonus for his allotment neighbours. "They might get the odd weed from my plot but they don't need pellets because my frogs eat tons of slugs. They're enthused by it all."

"Slugs are caviar to amphibians."

THERE'S ONIONS IN THEM THAR ALLOTMENTS

Allotmenteering is in Kevin and Jill's blood. For Kevin that's no problem, but for Jill it's taking a little time for her ancestry to assert itself.

Kevin is an artist; his family ran smallholdings. "So for me it's genetic. And there are similarities between working the plot and painting. You're outside of time... But I've yet to paint the shed door." Jill works as a theatre director; her family farmed in Italy. "I hadn't grown a thing before I met Kevin. The farming genes got lost somewhere. So now I'm learning how. And for me the allotment is like theatre, it's arranging space."

Inside the shed – celebrating its 40th birthday and a third move around the country – is a picture of Kevin's grandfather. "He looks like a pioneering Lee Marvin clutching bunches of onions... A real inspiration." The greenhouse is full of tomatoes and basil; the freezer is overflowing with homemade pesto.

"I'm learning... from the director's chair."

IT'S WHAT FRIENDS ARE FOR

Stan is living proof that the true spirit of allotmenteering is alive and very well. "If I hadn't had people around me to show me what to do and encourage me, I think I might have given up. Those people have become friends, good ones."

It's 26-year-old Stan's first season on the plot. It hadn't been touched in years but the "old boys" saw he was determined to have a go and helped him put up a shed and greenhouse, complementing his enthusiasm with barrow-loads of advice. Stan also had barrow-loads of manure from the stables he used to work at. "I could give some away as a 'thank you' for all the advice. Who needs books with these people around?"

Stan's daughter, Jasmine, reckons she's now a seasoned allotmenteer. "They're her sunflowers. Good, aren't they?" The team have been busy building tables and chairs from felled trees and a barbecue. "Next year will be great. We can't wait."

"We're one big happy family here."

LAST CALL FOR BLACKPOOL

When Little Kate fluttered into George's pigeon loft after flying 278 miles in just over five hours she did an awful lot for her owner's marriage. "I won £1,000 on that race and we spent it on a trip to Blackpool. The wife complains she doesn't see much of me so that made up for it."

In just nine years, 73-year-old George has become a successful pigeon racing man and from his power base on the allotments he has bred and trained big winners. There are other fanciers on George's site but not many tips are shared. Pigeon racing is a closed, secret world.

But George is prepared to reveal what he feeds the birds on – a corn called Versilaga Prestige. So how do Little Kate and her chums find their way back to their warm beds after a long, hard race? "*That* is Mother Nature's best kept secret."

"There's no one worse than pigeon men for jealousy."

AGE SHALL NOT WEARY THEM

Bryan has a problem. There's a waiting list for the allotments he helps run and it's not getting any shorter. "It's the old 'uns. They won't peg out. They're all too fit."

Running the "best fitness centre in town" has Bryan fighting off allotmenteering's old fogey image. "The tide is slowly turning. The younger element is getting involved, earnest about fresh, organic food."

Bryan has tended his plot for 34 years but reckons he visited the allotments before he was even born. "My grandfather gardened here and it was family tradition to walk from home, inspect the allotment, then go on to the pub." Although a fighting fit 66, Bryan lets his inventive streak take some of the strain. He has various solar-powered contraptions, including one that slowly reels in the hose as it waters the vegetables. "I'm a member of the Frank Whittle Appreciation Society. I know what inventors go through..."

"Allotments should be funded by the NHS."

61

I CAN SING A RAINBOW

Teresinha's city-centre allotment is a long way from Rio but it oozes the colour of carnival. Her Brazilian roots see to that. "I love my allotment and I love colour."

Teresinha and her husband, Mike – "He earns the pennies and I work the allotment" – have two plots. "Seeing the allotments from the bus, they looked exciting and untidy. We've made lots of friends. Our allotments are so cosmopolitan."

Gaudy pumpkins spill over one of her plots. "I like to put them all round the house and maybe I'll put on a show for the public some time." Flowers dominate the other allotment. And Teresinha's passion runs to growing dye-making plants. "I have woad, madder and weld; blue, red and yellow." But extracting the vivid blue dye from the woad in the traditional way was too much, even for her. "I've had to use chemicals. Using fermented urine was just too smelly."

"Getting on my allotment is better than going on holiday."

WE SHALL NOT BE MOVED

When a bulldozer was driven across Vic and his friends' church-owned allotments it was Round One of a five year holy war. "Who'd have thought gardeners would be fighting the church? It turned very nasty."

The land was ripe for development, but 79-year-old Vic and the allotmenteers staged sit-ins and protests – helped, ironically enough, by an academic named Christian – until the weight of the law saw them prosecuted and fined. The campaign, led by medics, lawyers, plumbers and carpenters, went on to a tribunal where the inspector ruled that the site should never be built on. All 22 allotments are now taken and there's a waiting list.

The spirit that saw off injustice has seen a Millennium Green created on the site with its own garden and playground, a stage for open-air concerts... and the planting of a special rose, New Dawn. Vic and his champions' battle cry was: "Here we stand. We can do no other," originally uttered by Martin Luther.

NEW DAWN

THIS ROSE WAS PLANTED
IN CELEBRATION
OF SAVING
T. STEPHEN'S ALLOTMENTS
OM THE BUILDERS' BULLDOZER

AUTUMN 1999

"We were the Christians,
they were the persecutors."

OH, WHAT A MARVELLOUS THING TO BE

...A busy, busy bee on John's and Andy's allotments. John confesses he's "not much of a gardener", so his allotment is all grass and bees, a couple of sheds and some ducks – to keep the grass down.

But what about those humans who aren't too keen on being stung? "I fly a flag to warn my neighbour I've disturbed the bees. But because bees don't like dark colours he's less likely to get 'buzzed' if he wears his white sun hat."

Down the way, Andy gets on with his three hives. "I have a placid type of bee and you usually only get stung if you're in the flight path." He also has some vegetables and rows of prolific fruit bushes, which help satisfy his passion for gooseberry pie. "You get into some funny scrapes with bees. You could say we are a little odd."

"You don't have to be mad to keep bees... but it helps."

DIG THIS!

Gary does more digging than most allotmenteers. Not only does he turn the sod on his plot but he also digs for a living – as an archaeologist with the National Trust.

From day one, four years ago, Gary was turning up pieces of olde England on his little piece of sceptred isle. "Deeper digging turns up all sorts," he says, "and, what my neighbours might chuck out, I hang on to and add to my collection."

The plots have been tilled since the 14th century. The ground was manured with all sorts of household waste and that sometimes included broken bits and pieces. So the ground is as rich in history as humus. Gary's finds include clay pipes from the 19th century, smashed pottery from much earlier – and the detritus of the 20th century. One piece of the past has come back to haunt him. He got rid of his traditional tumbledown shed to a friend, who recycled it. "It scowls at me across the allotments as my new shed splits in the sun."

"I suppose I have an eye for the stuff."

PIZZA AND POETRY

Watch Barbara when she goes to eat her pizza. She'll be giving the tomatoes the once over. In just two seasons, she's gone from being an allotment novice to secretary of her local plot holders' association, poet… and beef tomato expert. "It was really odd and no one believed me, but after cooking a frozen pizza I put the tomato pips to one side, let them dry, sowed them and produced the fattest, sweetest tomatoes you can imagine."

Barbara thanks her sister, Doreen, for introducing her to allotmenteering. "I used to go fishing with my husband but got fed up with it. Doreen had an allotment and I thought I'd give one a try and it escalated from there."

While Barbara digs, writes and organizes, she lives for her favourite dish – tomatoes, eggs and chips. She has to buy the eggs. "No livestock's allowed on the allotments, that's the rules… Sam stays in his dog hutch."

"My computer has no viruses,
but there are plenty of bugs on the allotment."

PROBLEM? WHAT PROBLEM?

"You don't have an excess of slugs, you have a duck deficiency." This refreshing way of looking at one of the allotmenteer's greatest headaches sustains Graham as he works his plot. He's a vegan-organic gardener, and a permaculturalist, committed to "designing sustainable human communities by following nature's patterns," or "turning problems into solutions."

When the local mayor suggested concreting over the allotments to provide much-needed parking for the hospital, Graham had the answer. "I told them to tear up the roads and turn them into even more allotments. The good food, fresh air and exercise provided by them would lessen the need for hospitals."

Though he recycles as much urban waste as possible, he's not working towards self-sufficiency. "Building a self-reliant community is probably a more practical aim." He's had his allotment 10 years and grows just about everything. But he can't grow carrots. Graham's answer to that problem? "I don't bother with them."

"I suppose you could call me a crank...
a healthy one, anyway."

CURTAIN UP ON THE GREEN ROOM

Allotments are conservative places. The seasons are about the only things that change. Unless, that is, you dig and plant alongside Tom. Then, to the strains of a wind-up gramophone, you can take part in a poetic discourse on the mating habits of snails.

Tom's experimental theatre, funded by the Arts Council, has been playing to a full allotment. "The audience meets at a pub, then they're ushered to the allotment where they're offered a feast of visual images, music, dance and the spoken word."

Up to 40 allotment-goers sit or wander as Tom and the team entertain among his marrows and beans. They might find a dancer buried up to her knees. One turn features the shed. "I had some whistling choristers and some singers, who appeared from hidden windows singing 'There is a Rose in Spanish Harlem'. I was on the roof throwing rose petals at the audience. It went down well."

"The local newspaper headline was *Tom loses the plot.*"

THE GREAT ESCAPE

"It's not just the growing of vegetables; it's being there." That's how award-winning garden designer, Cleve, sums up his love of his allotment. It's his chance of getting his hands dirty, away from impressing clients with patios in Oxford and a good few acres in Sunningdale. "Design is one thing, gardening is another. It's a chance to practise what I preach. There are too many in my game who don't."

Cleve and Christine – an artist who uses the plot for inspiration – took on their load of couch grass and bramble four years ago. They built a "wonky" shed with timber from rubbish skips, tamed the ground, and made a lot of friends. "It's designed to some extent. We have a few artistic nick-nacks around. Pieces of sculpture."

Among Cleve's more doubtful friends are the slugs. "I don't kill anything on the allotment. All the so-called pests have their rights. I am learning to plant and work around them."

"It's one of the few occasions I get to chill out."

A MAGICAL, MYSTICAL PLOT

The Magic Roundabout and *The Wizard of Oz* are the inspiration behind Julie and Lorraine's garden playground, which features a psychedelic apple tree and a scarecrow called Miss Artois.

Lorraine wanted to spread her gardening wings and took on an allotment. Friend Julie got involved and before they knew it they were hooked. So were Holly, Emily, Grace and Philip (pictured from left). "Everywhere we go we pick up decorations for the tree. Windmills, sunflowers and CDs – everything. Then we got a load of wood chippings, made paths with them, and then we had the yellow brick road, and Dorothy and her friends."

And Miss Artois? "We made a scarecrow and toasted her with a can of lager." The shed – "we think of it more as a beach hut" – provides even more colour. Gardening also gets a look in. "We've had more vegetables and tomatoes than we can cope with. Call it beginners' luck."

"Colour and fun."

SALUD!

Jesus knows how to make friends and influence people down on the allotments. A few bottles of house wine from his restaurant just along the road – and possibly a song – and he has all the advice he needs to keep a supply of super-fresh vegetables for the busy kitchen. "I have so many friends there. I teach them how to cook. They teach me how to grow vegetables."

Not one to miss out on publicity, Jesus wheels his produce through the town in a barrow to his restaurant, Costas. "I named it after the costas of Spain and Cumbria. Costa Brava and Costa Blanca in Spain. Costa lot to live here, in Cumbria."

Jesus left Spain eight years ago. He's been cooking 25 years and allotmenteering for four. "I love it, away from the stress. I have a stove in the shed and can get some paperwork done there. And I take bookings on the mobile phone."

"If a customer has a slug in their lettuce, they get that – and a pint – for free."

BLOW WAVES AND BOX

If James offers to cut your hair, keep an eye on him. His mind might just wander back to his passion – topiary – and leave you with a ball instead of a bob. "I'm gradually packing up as a hairdresser. I decided it was time for a change. I planted my allotment with box and yew and now topiary runs my life."

James is an authority on sculptural topiary. Using traditional sheep-shearing clippers he can turn out anything from balls and spirals to ducks and teddy bears. "The thing is, don't let it get too complicated. Keep it simple. Use your imagination and generate organic, amorphous shapes."

It seems that imagination has left his neighbours behind. "Allotment holders can be a pretty morose lot. They don't really react to my efforts and wonder why I don't just get with on growing vegetables." However, there are a few spuds growing alongside the *Phillyrea latifolia*.

**"My latest work is a bit experimental...
You could call it a bow-legged Martian."**

LOVE AT FIRST SITE

Chris began working life in a city council finance department, took a job in the allotment sites office because it offered a pay rise... and that was it. "I just fell in love with allotments. It was everything about them."

But the course of 32-year-old Chris's love affair didn't run smooth. "The old duffers used to say to me – the man from the council – 'What do you know about it?' And they were right. So I got myself an allotment and I felt I was one of them."

Then it was onward and upward. He's now part-time with the local authority and running his own landscaping business. "I'm on Age Concern's referral list to help older people who can't manage their gardens. It seems my dealing with the old allotment holders – the old duffers – helped me build up a rapport." But Chris still lives for getting on his own allotment and de-stressing, while girlfriend, Lisa, gives moral support. "She has a small herb plot."

"You could say I'm addicted."

BINGO VERSUS BRASSICAS

Enter Geordie, allotment left, wearing cloth cap and check shirt. His plot resembles a gardening theatre thanks to his wry sense of humour.

What was a blank fence between the plot and some buildings is now a beautifully painted backcloth with butterflies and birds, hanging baskets... and antlers. "I helped cut some big bushes down for a mate. What we were left with looked like antlers. So I stripped them and painted them and hung them up." In front of that is a pond – a cunningly disguised sunken bath complete with seals – then the business end of the operation: enough vegetables for family and friends.

It has worked, because the former miner and foundryman, who has tended his patch for around 30 years, has won the local best kept allotment competition three times. Patricia, Geordie's wife of the best part of 40 years, still wonders about the time he spends on the plot...

"But she has her bingo."

TRUE GRIT

Dougie's story is a sad one but also one of determination and that bond that keeps the allotment fellowship strong in the face of ready-packed recreation.

Dougie is 83. A retired Royal Airforceman, he uses those years of self-discipline and fitness to make the most of his plot in the face of destruction and disinterest. "The vandalism is really bad. The police say they haven't got the men, but they find them for football matches and things." Five greenhouses have been burnt down, but Dougie and the others work on, swapping yarns and reinforcing friendships. "We'll not be beat."

Dougie mulls it over as he digs the ground he has tended for 23 years, or works in his two greenhouses, which are linked by a shed in a classic example of allotment architecture. His replacement hip has slowed him down – "I take about half an hour to walk the mile to my allotment" – but he finds digging helps. A good half of the hundred or so plots are derelict – "a shame and a waste."

"You could say I'm one of the last of the die-hards."

NO STING IN THIS TALE

Gunars is a bit of an old softie. As a result he and his wife Jill have thousands of friends. During the summer they opened their allotment shed to a colony of wasps. "If we're honest they moved in before we could do much about it, but once they started setting up home we let them get on with it."

The wasps and the two academics got on well together until Gunars banged the shed with his wheelbarrow. That was it. Squadrons of angry wasps saw to it that discretion rather than valour ruled the day. Gunars barricaded the door shut and baled out. "In fact, we went to Mexico for a month and when we returned they'd gone."

The experience prompted a magazine article on the pros and cons of sharing an allotment with wasps, a super-efficient do-it-yourself lemonade bottle wasp trap, and a healthy respect for those black and yellow opportunists that can rival the spray gun at pest control.

**"God made the bees
but the devil made the wasps."**

SLEEP, PERCHANCE TO REAP

Mathew and his chum Mark share an allotment, a self-deprecating sense of humour and the sleep disorder, narcolepsy. "Our problem is that we fall asleep with just a few moments warning. On the allotment we can keep an eye on one another and our neighbours are on standby for collapsing cultivators."

The pair met through an internet narcolepsy support group and took on the overgrown plot just a few months back. They bought a shed and tools – "It's the first time either of us has done anything like this, it's so good to work outdoors" – and threw themselves at the mercy of the older allotmenteers.

"They've been great. Giving us plants and loads of advice, although each one that comes up seems to contradict the bloke before!" Mathew and Mark had a laugh about where they can have a nap if need be. "I'm going to grow some of that Japanese ornamental grass. Just the thing if we nod off."

You don't have to be Mad to Live here. But if you are,- it helps.

"To hell with the television."

ACKNOWLEDGEMENTS

For help with research and assistance, thanks go to the following individuals and organisations:

Steve Ambrose; Paul Archer (Rosedale & Victoria Allotments); John Baxter; Geordie Beck (Byker Allotments); Phil Bell (Brickfield Allotments); Nick Bellas (Penrith and District Allotments); Hannah Blake; Emma Bolton (Leeds City Council); Hilary Burden (Camden Council); Graham Burnett; Gordon Chester; Stephen Clampin (Bristol City Council); Melody Clark (Duxford Allotments); James Cooper (Cypress and Pleasant Street Allotments); James Crebben–Bailey; Amanda Cresswell (Evening Star); Joyce Earl; Neil Emery (Lancaster City Council); Lee Fish (Cambridge City Council); Caroline Foley; Tim Ford (Burley Model Allotments); Laura Forrester; Diane Gorrell (Chester County Council); Desmond & Carol Haines (Penrith and District Allotments); Susanna Harding; Jean Hind (Penrith and District Allotments); Peter Horrocks (Littlemoor Allotments); Derek Humphries; Judith Irwin (King George V Allotments); Dan Keech (Sustain); Gavin Keir (Seacroft Hall Allotments); Alan Marshall; Sarah McNicol; Adam Morris; Daniel Mountford (North West Counties Association of Allotment and Leisure Gardeners); Sinead Murphy; Annabel Other; Richie Partridge (Byker Allotments); Dick & Jenny Pearl (Old Chesterton Allotments); Helen Raper (Newcastle City Council); Paul Roberts (Beaumont Terrace Allotments); Linda Secker (Dorrington Road Allotments); Bill Smickersgill (Chapel Allerton Allotments); Dennis Smith; Sue Stokel-Walker; John Streeter (Alric Avenue Allotments); Bryan Taylor (Sidegate Lane Allotments); Barbara Wakefield (Clarkesfield Allotments); Janice Walters (Scarcroft Allotments); Anna Watson (Calderdale and Kirklees Food Futures); Cleve West; Clair Wild; Neil Wilson (Berwick-on-Tweed Borough Council); Richard Wiltshire (Research Officer, QED Allotments Group); David Woolley (Wigan Borough Council); Susan Wright (Burnley Borough Council).

First published in 2004 by
New Holland Publishers (UK) Ltd
London • Cape Town • Sydney • Auckland
www.newhollandpublishers.com

Garfield House
86–88 Edgware Road
London W2 2EA
United Kingdom

80 McKenzie Street
Cape Town 8001
South Africa

14 Aquatic Drive
Frenchs Forest, NSW 2086
Australia

218 Lake Road
Northcote, Auckland
New Zealand

10 9 8 7 6 5 4 3 2 1

ISBN 1 84330 497 X

Editor: Gareth Jones
Editorial Direction: Rosemary Wilkinson
Designer: Paul Wright @ Cube
Photographers: John Baxter, Laura Forrester

Reproduction by Modern Age Repro House Ltd,
Hong Kong
Printed and bound by Craft Print International
Pte Ltd, Singapore.

PHOTOGRAPHIC CREDITS

John Baxter: Cover – Front, Back (Top, Middle-
Bottom, Bottom); pp 2; 6; 8–9; 11; 18–21;
24–25; 28–31; 36–39; 42–47; 50–53; 56–59;
62–63; 66–67; 70–71; 78–81; 86–89; 91; 96.

Laura Forrester: Cover – Spine, Back (Middle-
Top); pp 5; 7; 10; 12–17; 22–23; 26–27; 32–35;
40–41; 48–49; 54–55; 60–61; 64–65; 68–69;
72–77; 82–85; 92–93.

Gunars Ulmanis: pp 90.